The Secret Formula For Success

Discover The Reason for your failures,
master the 6 secret steps to achieve
anything you want

Alex Silva

Do visit my website to read on my latest updates

Thealexsilva.com

Why I Wrote This Book

From an early age, I was fascinated by people who constantly achieved massive success in different areas of life. From entrepreneurs to spiritual guides, I wanted to know what was the secret formula.

After studying hundreds of role models, I found out that all of them follow the same steps in acquiring what they want. These specific steps create The Formula For Success.

Subsequently, I tried The Formula For Success on my personal life, the outcome (Results) were amazing, I could understand the bigger picture, therefore I could reformulate my strategy every time i bumped into a dead end!

I wrote this book so that people can take advantage of all the resources of the world and utilize them in their own personal life, without taking years of trial and error.

Subsequently, I tried The Formula For Success on my personal life, the outcome (Results) were amazing, I could understand the bigger picture, therefore I could reformulate my strategy every time i bumped into a dead end!

I wrote this book so that people can take advantage of all the resources of the world and utilize them in their own personal life, without taking years of trial and error.

Why You Should Read This Book

I can tell you that I had to dig deep and study everything I could get my hands on, I read hundreds of books, attended several seminars and watched countless hours of digital courses, and, of course, the worst pain was all those years of trial and error.

I usually say that the price of excellence is ten thousand hours (Yes, 10 000).

Think of the thousands of hours of research time you will save by reading this book. You certainly could do the research yourself and come up with a formula, but you don't have to. I did the research for you, so that you cut short your learning curve and achieve success way faster because time is limited. From the day we are born we have a limited time to live, get the edge over life!

You can see how The Formula For Success presented in this book can be worth thousands or even hundreds of thousands of dollars.

Knowing this Formula always reminds me of a movie quote. Have you ever seen the movie Limitless? At the beginning of the movie Bradley Cooper said, 'I was blind but now I see'. This is how I felt after knowing and applying this formula to my own life.

Table of Contents

Chapter 1. Introduction

All my life, I always asked myself, 'How can some people experience so much wealth in their life, while others live a life of poverty?' 'I wonder If there is a formula for success?' at this point I knew little or nothing about finances and accounting but I always heard or perhaps read somewhere that the successful people do similar things.

Then, I started to ask myself 'Is there a pattern that I can analyze that enables regular people to become successful?'. The next step for me was obvious, I needed to study my ass off so I could identify some patterns, so I started studying hundreds of role models, people like Anthony Robbins, Richard Branson, Jeff Bezos, Bill Gates, Warren Buffett, etc. Anything I could get my hands on I would devour it! From books, seminars, courses, and many others. Although they act in different areas, for example,

Warren Buffett built his wealth from investing in Stocks while Bill Gates built his wealth through Microsoft. But they all take the same steps to get what they want. It doesn't matter if they made their fortune in Stocks, or Options, or real estate, or being an entrepreneur. They all follow a pattern.

There are six major steps. Follow this success formula, and you will be able to achieve anything you want. Miss any of these steps, and your dreams will never become the reality that you deserve.

Chapter 1. Step one of The Formula For Success

Know your Outcome

In virtually any situation of life, you have to decide what you want. The clearer In what you want, the clearer your brain gets it, therefore it is easier for your brain to come up with alternative answers, you must get focused in want you want.

The sad part is that people never seem to get what they want or they are not clear about it.

So many people go through their life just getting whatever they get, getting whatever comes to them, and the reality is that if you want to become a successful individual, you got to know what do you want, you need to know what your dreams are, you must figure it out, not only in terms of your dreams but in all areas of your life.

If you don't have a specific target, you cannot develop an effective strategy to get there.

How can knowing your outcome help you? When you know your outcome, you are able to empower yourself. Let me give you a simple example, 'Have you ever got caught in an argument and the only thing you wanted is to be right and win the argument? Even if winning the argument could cause problems?'. We all at one point in time did this. If you asked yourself 'what's my outcome?' you probably come up with an answer to wanting to resolve things instead of arguing.

Start developing the habit of asking yourself, 'What's my outcome?' 'What do I want specifically out of this situation?'. Most people when they are stuck in a challenge, they only see that challenge in front of them. Asking these questions will redirect your focus, and in life, we tend to get what we focus on. If you focus on the problem, what are you going to get? The problem, right? If you ask these questions over and over again, your brain starts to give you alternatives that you never had before. You empower yourself to create a new scenario!   If there is some area of

your life that is not working for you

(could be your career, your relationships,

health) keep asking yourself 'what's my

outcome in this area?'.

Let me give you another example, this time a more specific one. Let's say your salary now is $2,000 and you want to increase it. First, you need to specify how much you want to increase it by, If you wanted $20,000, you need to increase your income by 10x. Second, you have to give it a time span. So, your goal is to increase your income from $2,000 to $20,000 in twelve months. You need to be specific about what you want, saying that you want to increase your income it is just not enough. You need to be very specific.

I can tell you from all the books I read, success never happens by chance, most of it happens by knowing what they want and then apply it to real life. The sad part is most people rarely know what they want or are never specific about it.

Tiger woods set his goal of becoming the world's number one golfer! 13 years later he achieved his goal by the age of 21. How? He spent 13 years focusing on his game in order to take it to the level he needed in order to be the best.

I usually say this, doesn't matter how old or how young you are, doesn't matter if you are poor or if you have a Twenty million dollar net worth, you need to set specific goals on what you want to achieve in all areas of life.

Chapter 2. Step two of The Formula For Success

Develop a Strategy

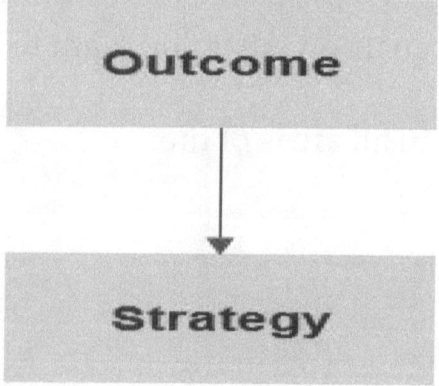

After knowing what you want (your outcome), you need to know how to get there. In other words, you need a Plan/Strategy. How do we develop a strategy? (Down below, I will teach you a technique that you can utilize to develop an effective strategy and to shorten your learning curve in 1/3 of the time), First, we need to understand what a strategy is.

A strategy is a sequence of steps that consistently produces a specific result. It's no different from a recipe. If you want to bake a cake, you need a specific order of things; you need to have all the ingredients, you need to get a bowl, crack the eggs, preheat the oven, etc. The outcome is the cake, the strategy is the series of steps to get there. What would happen if you left one of the steps out? For example, you forgot to get a bowl. You obviously wouldn't get your outcome. People have 'recipes' for everything they do, people have strategies for Love, wealth, decisions, for making a purchase, for motivation, etc. It is a specific series of steps that you run through in order to produce that behavior, it could be a series of thoughts that produce the behavior!

Any type of habits you have are strategies that you have. Why is this important? Because our actions determine our destiny and our actions are mainly unconscious, have you ever found yourself doing some behavior without any conscious thought? And wondered why you were doing it?. That's because you were running an unconscious strategy. This applies to every aspect of your life!

Are your strategies consistent with the goals that you want to accomplish or not?

What if I told you that you can develop an effective strategy and speed up dramatically the process of success? We call the process modeling.

For example, if you want to learn how to play soccer and you knew nothing about it, it may take you a while for you to be able to get the techniques and all the necessary skills, in other words, It would take time to create the necessary thought patterns and the neuro-connections to produce that result.

Through the process of modeling, we can find someone who is really good at playing soccer, and then we can learn how does he mentally wire his brain to produce the results that we want. We elicit the person's strategy and install it within ourselves so that we can cut short all those years of trial and error.

If we replicate a person's mental blueprint, we can replicate their success, imagine this, if we could replicate the way they think, the way they behave, the way they carry themselves, we can produce the same results they produce.

If you were to practice with Cristiano Ronaldo, and you knew how he trains, how he thinks, what is he thinking while playing, you could replicate his success.

Now, would you be Cristiano Ronaldo? Of course not, he has years and years of experience, but one thing is for sure, you would be able to shorten your learning curve massively.

Let's take another example, public speaking. Public speaking is the number one fear in the world, so wouldn't it be great if you could walk on stage and deliver a speech with ease and confidence? Guess what, you can.

NLP was created as a result of Modeling.

Bandler and Grinder's system for

Modeling was essentially to discover

somebody's belief systems, physiology,

and mental strategies.

4 steps of Modeling

Step 1- Identify a model of excellence

Step 2- Observe how this person moves, breathes (deep or shallow?), behaves, gestures (Big gestures or small gestures? Fast or slow gestures?). Observe how he uses his posture, observe his tone of voice (high or low pitch? Fast or slow? raspy or clear?) observe is facial expressions (facial tension or relaxed?)

Step 3 – Image in your mind what would it be like to be this person, step in the shoes of this person, and mentally rehearse. How would you react to the events in your personal life if you were him/her? How would you move, breathe, walk, act, behave, speak?

Step 4 – Physically do it. Become this person, getting the same results he's getting, mimic his physiology, and really associate. Have fun doing this.

Different goals require different strategies

The other thing that you need to understand is that different goals require completely different strategies.

For instance, let's say that you own a restaurant and you are making roughly $2,000 a month in revenue.

You set a goal for $3,000 a month. What kind of strategy could you develop? You could increase your hours of labor, you could redo the menu so that could increase the number of clients, simple, right? Given the same situation, what if you set a goal for 1 Million dollars a month? The strategy had to be very different. Instead of having one restaurant, you probably would need multiple franchised restaurants.

The key lesson here is that there is no impossible, its only a matter of having the right strategy!

Chapter 3. Step three of The Formula For Success

Take Consistent Action

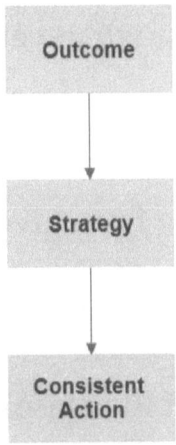

The third step consists in taking consistent action towards your goals. Now, I believe that there is an enormous difference between taking action and taking **consistent action**.

Taking action only leads you to the first dead-end road and you stop immediately, taking consistent action is making sure that whatever strategy you follow works or doesn't work.

The best analogy I can give you is in trading (and I had the exact same problem), one of the reasons why people lose in trading is because they assume the performance of a strategy based on the law of small numbers, they don't allow their statistic sample to be large enough so it can be accurate.

For you to know if a strategy is profitable you need to do at least 100 trades (consistent action), but people give up when they reach 10 or 20 (action), of course knowing that on a microscopic level (On a trade by trade level), each outcome is random and uncertain, however, on a macroscopic level (after doing many trades based on a consistent routine that gives you an edge), the aggregate outcome of many %-multiples should be positive. With this, I Am not saying that you keep trying the same thing forever and ever, what I Am saying is that you need to have a sizable number of experiences that know what works and does not work.

People often tell me one of two things: ' I don't have a clue what to do' or 'what if I try and It doesn't work?', I typically say that if you tried, and it didn't work, you got feedback and if you think about it you are better off now because you know what doesn't work and probably you learned a couple of new things that will help to leverage your success road.

And if you don't like where you are right now in your life, simple, decide that you want to change your life! A decision is very powerful when it comes to change. Do you know someone who may be less talented and intelligent than you are but is a lot more successful? No? C'mon, don't lie!!

We all know or knew someone like this, and do you know why they are more successful? You may be smarter, but they take a lot more consistent action and that is why they get a lot more results! So why do so many intelligent people fail to take consistent action? One big word: FEAR. Their fear of rejection, their fear of success, their fear of failure, their fear of everything. The only way to deal with fear is (you guessed it) facing it, look at eye to eye and keep taking action no matter how scary it seems.

There is a famous phrase that categorizes F.E.A.R perfectly, Fear is <u>False Evidence Appearing Real</u>.

What drives our actions are the emotional states that we experience. It is not what we can do in life that makes us successful, it is what we will do.

Fear, when controlled, can be very motivating, and it can be controlled like anything else in life.

It's like going to the gym, if you try to lift a heavyweight in your first day you probably will not be able do to it, but after a couple of months of consistent training, what happens? You can lift that same heavyweight with ease.

Chapter 4. Step Four of The Formula

For Success

Have behavioral flexibility

Once you know what you want, you have a strategy and you are taking consistent action do your actions always work? Of course not, most people fail more than succeed, in fact, successful people fail seven out of ten times, could you imagine having only a 30% window to succeed? That's why they are successful.

If you are not producing the results you want from your actions, you got fine tune your awareness, because if you are not being effective what are you going to do? You need to change your approach.

There are only two outcomes, the first possible outcome is that you experience success by moving towards or achieving your goal, the other possibility is that you encounter a dead-end road, is what we denominate as a failure.

As you know, you are more likely to encounter failure than success, so you need to know what to do when you get there. What do high achievers do? There are basically three approaches in which people deal with failure.

Approach #1 – Giving power to external events

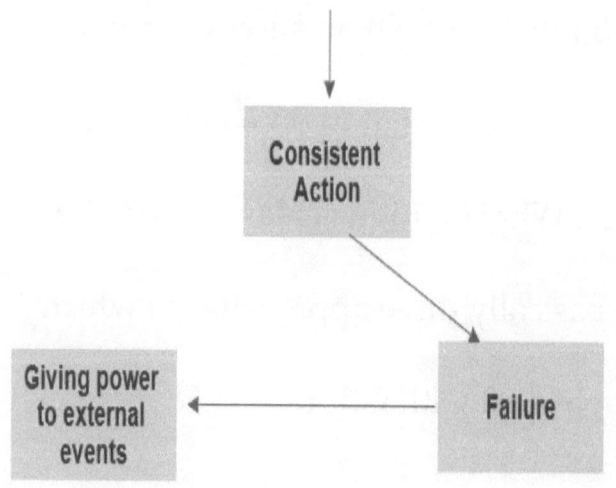

This first approach is when they encounter failure and they give all types of excuses why it did not work, blaming everyone else.

They say things like ' I can't do it', 'I'm just not smart enough', ' I have bad luck', 'I'm too young' or 'I'm too old', 'My dog distracted me', My cat distracted me' they blame anyone and everyone.

Probably one of the most popular phrases that exhibit this approach is 'the poor economy affected me'. What do you think will happen? You become powerless and your brain start's to associate more pain to continue than to achieve your goal, therefore, you will stop taking action and give up!

It's time to turn things around by becoming aware. Write down all the instances where you exhibit this first approach.

_____

_____

_____

_____

_____

_____

You now discovered some of your
potential goals that you gave up on them
by giving power to external events.

Approach #2 – Keep
Trying blindingly

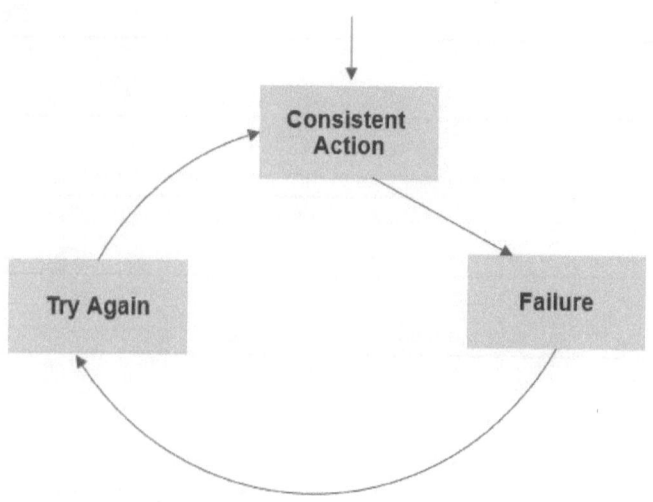

This second approach is when they don't get their desired outcome, they will not quite. They will get themselves to take action again and again.

They have a lot more determination but they have this mentality of not achieving the outcome because they didn't try hard enough or if 'I keep trying, I eventually will succeed'.

They will keep trying to take action, putting in more time and energy. No matter how many failures they encounter, they stick with it! Do they eventually achieve their outcome? Well, yes and no, it depends, there is a slight chance that if they set incremental goals, they learn from the small mistakes, and eventually, they might reach their outcome, but only if the goal is small!

Let's get back to our restaurant example, you make $2,000 a month in revenue.

You set a goal for $3,000 a month. Can you achieve it with this approach? You might, because the goal is not that far away from your current status (this is what we call incremental goal).

However, if the goal is to achieve $1,000,000.00, They may experience a better result, but they won't reach the desired goal. Why? Although they may experience slightly better results, they don't change their strategy, if you keep doing the same thing, you will get the same results you always got, and this works for every aspect of life.

There was a friend of mine who works as a real estate agent, although he's been there for only 3 years, he could only sell four houses in these 3 years, his goal was to achieve the highest sales volume in specific months of the year, but after two years of keep trying and failing, he eventually gave up, and said ' I just can't do it', so he came to me and asked why he rarely could sell anything. After going through all of his statistics, I noticed that he exhibited this approach, most of his leads came from cold calling, but his conversion rate was very poor, he was doing the same thing over and over again, so what did he get? The same results!

After redoing only his cold calling scripts, he saw a significantly higher conversion rate. After 6 months he achieved the highest sales volume three months in a row.

Plus, he got a company car and his own agent. So, you see what happened here? He kept trying the same strategy over and over again with the attitude of 'if I keep trying, I eventually will succeed', inevitably, the constant failure lead him to give up and to start having limiting beliefs about himself.

Like this example, there are many others, I see so many business people and salespeople who put in more time and energy every month without significantly increasing their sales! Why? Again, they keep using the same ineffective strategy, could be that they are targeting the same wrong costumers, making ineffective presentations, using ineffective scripts, or even keep trying to push sales forcefully.

There is only so much failure that a person could take, after a while, they start to get frustrated and disappointed, eventually, they develop limiting beliefs and it's a downhill spiral from there on. Write down all the instances where you exhibit this second approach.

_____

_____

_____

_____

_____

_____

Approach #3 – Get Feedback, Change Strategy and Take consistent action until you succeed

So, what is the last approach that all high achievers exhibit? When they don't achieve their outcome, they don't see it as a failure, they see it as feedback or a learning experience.

They then learn from the feedback and they immediately change their strategy and take consistent action again.

What if they fail again? They keep repeating this cycle until they get the results they want.

Remember failing is an option, if you keep taking consistent action and changing your strategy, you eventually will get to your desired outcome. So, if you encounter failure, perceive it as feedback, change strategy, and keep taking consistent action!

Stephen King that today sold more than 400 million copies of his books was once living in a trailer with his wife, broke and desperate, King received so many rejections that he started to collect them. In his book On Writing, he recalls: "*By the time I was 14...the nail in my wall would no longer support the weight of the rejection slips impaled upon it. I replaced the nail with a spike and kept on writing.*". He received more than 60 rejections before selling his first story.

Another example was Thomas Edison. He took almost 10,000 attempts before inventing the light bulb. When asked how he did it, he said, '*I have not failed. I've just found 10,000 ways that won't work*.' What did he do? He used the feedback to change his strategy until he got what he wanted.

Another example was Mark Cuban, he is the owner of Dallas Mavericks, however, Mark Cuban failed in almost every job that he was employed, did he give up?

No! He changed his strategy and took massive consistent action! He is now worth 4 Billion dollars.

This is essentially the Formula for Success!!

These four steps will create massive success in your life!

These four steps will create massive success in your life!

Let's recap.

1- Know YOUR outcome

2- Develop a Strategy

3- Take consistent action

4- Have behavioral flexibility

You are probably saying 'that's it? Well, again, yes and no, I could teach this formula to many people, but few will put it to use. Why? There are two additional crucial elements that you will have to master in order to achieve a successful life. These elements are called our Values and our Beliefs.

Chapter 5. Step Five of The Formula For Success

Values

The first of these elements is called our values!

Your values influence that little voice in your head that tells you whether or not to care about something and how you should prioritize your time

All of us regard values like 'success',
'freedom', 'security', 'love', and
'happiness' very differently.

The important thing is that whatever our
values are, they must be aligned with our
goals.

Values are simply, what's most important
to us, they drive all upfront motivation.

Let me ask you something, what do you
rather have? And you could only pick
one.

1) Passion
2) Success
3) Happiness

4) Adventure

5) Love

It's different for everyone. Some people value success more than love, others value happiness more than success. Everyone in life learned to take different emotions and give them levels of importance.

Take someone for example that values success and does not value love, this means that if this person had to choose between a business meeting or a family dinner, they would choose the business meeting because they value success.

And vice versa, given the same situation. If someone valued love and does not value success, they would've said something along the lines of 'My family is everything, work comes next'.

So, you have to ask yourself what key values drive you in life?

Are you driven by success, security, freedom, God, friendship, love, power? Think about this and write down five of the most important values in your life. Ask yourself the following questions, 'What's more important to me in life? Why do I do what I do? What drives me as a person?

Remember that values are stated in the form of emotional states. For example, if you write down 'money', money is not an emotional state, ask yourself, 'what does 'Money' give you? Power, Freedom, security, etc. Same with family.

My Values

1_____

_____

_____

2_____

_____

_____

3_____

_____

_____

4_____

_____

_____

5_____

_____

_____

Ok, great! Once you know what your values are, you know what motivates you unconsciously! You have to use them to drive you towards your goals. This is very important, your values must be aligned with your goals, if this step is not right, you would probably procrastinate so much that you eventually give up or don't start at all.

Chapter 6. Step Six of The Formula For Success

Beliefs

The second element is called our Believes!

In any given time we receive about 2

million bits of information per second via

our 5 senses, but it is physically

impossible for our nervous system to

cope with all of it.

So, our mind filters all of this information by deleting, distorting, and generalizing all this information to an internal representation of what is actually happening around us.

In simple English, we never see reality, we perceive a filtered version of reality.

This is the reason why 2 people can have the same experience but have a totally different reality about it.

I remember a couple of years ago going to a comedy show, the show had a delay of 30 minutes and the comedian was known for his ethnicity jokes. This show for me was one of the funniest comedy shows I ever saw, the jokes were amazing, the crowd was laughing and the setup was just perfect. Now, my partner had a completely different opinion. She said that the jokes were a bit 'too much', she complained a lot about the delay and said that the crowd was making too much noise.

You see, we went to the same show, heard the same comedian but our interpretations of reality were totally different.

Beliefs are generalizations that you made about different aspects of your life, believes determine how we perceive the world and how we respond to the events around us, they determine what we will or will not do, what we will or will not try.

For example, have you ever had a wrong generalization (Belief) about a certain person and then when you start a conversation with her your brain just went 'I don't know about this person, let me be cautious', just to discover that the belief you had about this person was completely wrong? The beliefs about a person will determine how you interact with that person, whether you go out and make friends or avoid that person.

The beliefs you have about a particular food will determine if you eat that food or not.

Your beliefs drive your goals, what you believe in, in yourself and other aspects of life, will determine what you want in life! What you want if life will determine your strategies and your actions, your beliefs will also determine what you will do when you encounter failure, do you treat it as feedback or will you give up.

So, Let's start by asking yourself 'What limiting beliefs do I have?' Revisit your past experiences and think for a moment of all possible beliefs that have been limiting your life all these years.

Limiting Beliefs act on the unconscious level so they can be tricky to uncover!

I am going to give you two different strategies so that you can uncover your limiting beliefs!

Here are some examples of limiting beliefs:

'Money is the root of all evil'

'Money Doesn't grow on trees'

'No one wants me'

'I will never find love'

'I am not talented'

'I'm not smart enough'

'Everyone else in my family is overweigh'

What are the beliefs that are limiting your life now?

What beliefs do you have that could be preventing you from realizing your full potential and live the life that you always dreamed of?

What are your beliefs about people?

About money? Your own capabilities?

Your career? About the world? About

relationships? About growth? About

business?

First Strategy

I want you to take all the time you need

and list down all the limiting beliefs that

you have in the different areas of your

life.

Consider your beliefs about: Yourself, People, Love, Relationships, Life, Learning, Career, Success, Spiritual growth.

1._____

_____

_____

2._____

_____

_____

3._____

_____

_____

4._____

_____

_____

5._____

_____

_____

6._____

_____

_____

7._____

_____

_____

Second Strategy

The second strategy it's about knowing your ultimate goals (I do encourage you to read my book, Goal Setting Workshop, so you know what you want to create in the next 10 to 15 years of your life) and then write why won't you already achieved your goal.

Describe a situation/Goal you're struggling with and add the word 'Because' at the end of it.

Example:

I can't start a business because _____.

I can't start a business **because I am not smart enough.**

I can't start a business because **I don't have enough money.**

In these two statements, **I am not smart enough** & **I don't have money** are your limiting beliefs!

For me, this second strategy works the best, it's simple and effective! Combining the two can be very powerful!

Now, once you uncovered your limiting beliefs, run them into the next following worksheet!

Limiting beliefs about Yourself	How has it cost you?	How will it cost you in the Future?
1.		
2.		
3.		
4.		

Limiting beliefs about People & Relationships	How has it cost you?	How will it cost you in the Future?
1.		
2.		
3.		
4.		

Limiting beliefs about Life & Success	How has it cost you?	How will it cost you in the Future?
1.		
2.		
3.		
4.		

Limiting beliefs about Money	How has it cost you?	How will it cost you in the Future?
1.		
2.		
3.		
4.		

Process of changing Beliefs

Step 1- Associate enough pain to the limiting belief.

• Decide that it MUST change!

Step 2- Challenge the references that

support the limiting belief.

- What else could it mean?

- Find counter examples

_____

_____

_____

Step 3- Create a new empowering belief

_____

_____

_____

Step 4- Create new references to back up

this new belief

_____

_____

_____

Step 5- Associate enough pleasure to the

new belief

_____

_____

_____

Step 6- Future Pace

• How would this new belief change

your life and your success?

_____

_____

_____

Anytime you want to change a limiting

belief, come back to this Process! Feel free

to assist someone else to break free from

their limiting beliefs by using this

process.

The Secret Formula for Success

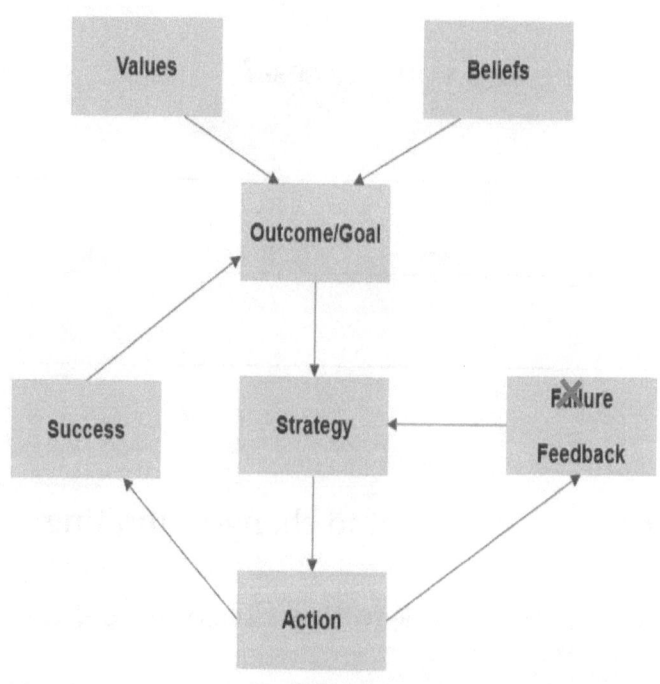

The Secret Formula for Success is the most powerful process you can utilize to achieve whatever you want!

The next big question to ask yourself is 'Are you committed to succeed?', there is a significant difference between wanting to achieve success and a desire.

For most people wanting to be successful, having more freedom, having more money is just a desire, they can live without it! As a result, they never take action because something more important will always come up to fill up their time.

When a goal is just a desire or a wish, you will find yourself procrastinating and being held back by frustration and failures.

You see, when a goal is a weak desire you will never dare to get out of your comfort zone and if you don't get out of your comfort zone, you will never grow. You make up all kinds of excuses for not doing it. In the end, you will never do whatever it takes to get what you want.

About 4 years ago, when I started my self-development journey, I had this fear of rejection, this fear held me back and stopped me from stepping out of my comfort zone, even though, deep inside I knew that was the only option for growth. After learning how to control my emotions, I then had the courage to get out of my comfort zone and only then I started to grow. The key ingredient to start and continue my self-development journey was COMMITEMENT!

I was committed to do whatever it took to experience a breakthrough in my life, I believe that only 5% of people are committed to succeed, the rest of the 95% will just hope to achieve success.

Let me give you an extreme example, have you ever set a goal to lose weight? Most people will say yes. What happens in the first couple of days/weeks? You are probably very excited and motivated, but soon you give up and fail to achieve your outcome, right? You say things like 'I don't have time', or I don't have the discipline'. What happened if I told you that you had to lose 5 kg (11 pound) in a short period of time or I would kill your beloved one, would you be able to do it? I bet you would.

So, what was the difference (aside from the killing part), you are you, you were always been you! You ALWAYS had the resources and capabilities to achieve any goal. We just lack the MUST!

When a goal becomes a MUST, we operate from a very different mindset, with just a shift in thinking we tap into our unlimited personal resources and this enables us to achieve virtually anything we want!

IS YOUR ROAD TO SUCCESS A 'WISH' OR A 'MUST'?

Last assignment

Were there instances when you achieved
your outcome by getting feedback and
changing your strategy? Write down at
least four of these instances.

_____

_____

_____

_____

_____

In what specific areas of your life can you begin putting into practice the ultimate success formula to help you get what you want?

_____

_____

_____

_____

One Last Thing…

If you enjoyed this book or found it useful I'd be very grateful if you'd post a short review on Amazon. Your support really does make a difference and I read all the reviews personally so I can get your feedback and make this book even better.

Thanks again for your support!

About The Author

Alex Silva is the author of The Goal Setting Workshop. He lives in Leiria, Portugal. Alex loves educating and inspiring other authors and entrepreneurs to succeed and live the life of their dreams.

Learn more about Alex at www.thealexsilva.com

Learn more about Alex at amazon.com/author/thealexsilva